The Still Room

by

Shirley Bell

New and Selected Poems
chosen by Dave Kavanagh

THE
BLUE
NIB

The Still Room

by
Shirley Bell

New and Selected Poems
chosen by Dave Kavanagh

First published in Great Britain in 2018 by The
Blue Nib

ISBN 978-1-9999550-3-8

With thanks to Dave Kavanagh

for choosing the poems in this collection

Introduction

I first encountered Shirley in the summer of 2017 when she submitted work to our then fledgling magazine, The Blue Nib. It was an easy decision to select her as our featured poet that week and further, to ask her to lend a hand with the magazine. To my delight Shirley was quick to step into the role of Editor-in-Chief and has since taken responsibility for selecting content. Her attention to quality and detail become clear to any who peruse The Blue Nib.

In December 2017 Shirley sent me her collected works, *Dark is a Way and Light is a Place*, which I read over the Christmas break. I enjoyed the book so much that I took it with me on my annual writing binge in January and it remained on my bedside locker for the duration, becoming more and more dog-eared. In fact, over the three months of intensive writing, it was the one book I returned to repeatedly. Shirley's talent is in her ability to condense a story and turn it into a poem that resonates with readers on several levels, so the poetry demands re-reading.

She explores life in all its strength and fragility, all of it presented through an eye that observes the unseen detail and in a way that allows the reader to immerse themselves.

We not only read Shirley's work, we live with it, and with the joy and the pain expressed. She is often humorous, sometimes self-deprecating, but always a poet.

She writes from the standpoint of a mother, a wife, a warrior and a human. When I selected the poems for this collection, I had the enormous pleasure of re-reading previous work and reading, for the first time, new work. I found I learned more with each reading, so that the poetry felt like a skin one could slip into with ease.

It is a pleasure to know Shirley both through her work and as a friend. I leave you knowing you too will live with and love the poetry of Shirley Bell.

Dave Kavanagh
28th May 2018.

New Poems
2016 – 2018

Tell it to the bees

The garden hums. Bees guzzle in the throats
of the lush flowers and butterflies clot the blossoms.
The simple flowers are full of nectar. Sometimes
the hives are dressed in mourning. Someone has
rapped softly and told it to the bees. Their hive servant
who managed their perfect world has gone.

As the coffin settles in its grave, so gentle hands
lift and set down the colony with its waxen cells
like catacombs. And reverently, lay out their share of
funeral meats and drinks at the entrance where the bees
dance their maps; carry the pollen in their baskets
to feed the hive in their secret waxen chambers.

Cells dripping with nectar metamorphosing into honey:
that gold that gives the gift of prophecy. Telling the bees.
But there is a stutter in the rituals. Threats grow like
the larvae in those perfect hexagons. The doubled flowers
flounce their skirts. Nectarless. The bees in their quietened hive
are alive instead with Varroa mites, crawling in their plush.

And all the words of prophecy roll on the tongue.
Foul Brood and Nosema,
Colony Collapse and neonicotinoids.

Tell it to the bees.

The Lady Chapel and the Virgin

You have been my harbour.
Safe as stone, quiet
as the grave slabs beneath
my feet. I have wept here

for my damaged vessels;
filled them with hope
and tears. Then
everything was inundated.

The sea spilled itself
and filled you up. Kneelers
bobbed along the aisles.
Today there is no altar

in the Lady Chapel, it is
flotsam, and two gilded angels
are sulking back to back.
But it has been rinsed clean.

And she is still standing,
with a candle at her feet.
Her face is as mild as milk
and her infant's face is

carved with light.

Full cold moon on Christmas Eve

It's a full moon on Christmas Eve. It hangs above
the blackness of the quiet rooftops, the frantic scribble
of bare branches and the Christmas lights that climb
the walls, surround the window panes, and light the trees
inside, illuminating the waiting packages intermittently.

Its frosted face is pocked with the impact
of all those meteors and the tiny tracks of adventurers,
I suppose. I don't recall seeing this before, so I hesitate
on the step, my key in the door, my son's dogs
howling with their broken loneliness. I, too, am lonely tonight.

But my solitude is as intermittent as those lights and this moon.
I look it up. It's called the "full cold moon", for December.
But it last appeared on Christmas Eve in 1977 and won't come
again until 2034. It's special then. I think of stockings, presents
and the house, full of family I'm ashamed I didn't always want to see.

This year I'm dodging Christmas. So all the ads are strangely
unimportant, as are the shoppers, frantic in Tesco.
And like the moon, I'm on the outside, looking in. Somewhere,
someone is going to be born tonight and will lie, fists in mouth, in
the arms of its tired mother. Like any other dying god.

Dr White

Dr. White, last time I came you were counting on your
fingers. "Four and twenty blackbirds," you said, "baked
in a pie" that just you could see. "You are only as old
as the woman you feel." No-one answered. "And that's a joke,"
you told us, sadly, but no-one got it.

Today you are rocking and reciting. It is poetry.
My mother says, "Hello," and so does Dr. White.
"Hello, hello. Hello. Go so, go low, go slow. NO!"
And, "Where? there?" "Would you? Should you? Would you?"
Then, "Go!" says Dr. White again and I'm wishing that I could.

But I have only been here for twenty minutes. A carriage clock,
its mechanism slow as treacle, turns to and fro, sealed in its case.
A DVD of *Pearl Harbour* is cycling through the start page. "*Play*"
it instructs us. Or "*Pick a Scene.*" Every now and then a plane flies
across the screen. Dr. White is shouting, "NO, NO" he says.

He is surrounded by etiolated women, sitting in special chairs.
Their necks are stretching towards whatever light remains.
"Shut up" they say, often, severally, but Dr. White just goes on
and on, rocking and chanting his dreadful incantations.
"Shall I hit him with my book?" my Mother says, and laughs.

Now I say "NO, NO", to her, and I sound like Doctor White.
Violet tells me what a wonderful doctor he was. I look
at his long, clever fingers and his wits are pouring through them,
and joining the other memories lost from all these fogged heads.

I can hear him when I leave. "Where? he is saying. "Where?"

Several Tests of Dementia Severity*

100   and all is clear and transparent
 I know my name
93   my name is isador browne ansell muth matio finnerty
an artificial construct legion or noigel even
86   this is a watch and this is a pencil
with the pencil I draw a watch face
79   it is the 26th november 2012 it is 11.15 am
on a fine spring day in 2012 in autumn
72   I have told you this
no ifs ands or buts
65   I read close your eyes and
I close my eyes no read it
59 no 58   what is your name I write what is your name
but you will not answer
51   and is a table like an orange like a dog
I live in this dlrow which is world backwards
44 and 37   say the objects
the objects
37 or 44 did I pass
you are you you cannot pass or fail
30   I I I say the world is creeping away
it is the dlrow now
23   is a banana like a bookcase and a horse
what is your name what is my name
23   I close my eyes
I do not want to read
23   no buts or ands or ifs
it is 16.15 on a dark day in November or 15.16
16 /9 in 2012 which I write with my pencil
while consulting my watch

2 I draw on my watch with my licnep

0 I have no nam

*www.stanford.edu/~ashford/MMSgenealogy/Several%20tests.doc

Autumn Is Coming

It's September and the sombre clouds are rolling
themselves up into tentative shapes, faces that
billow, then pass into oblivion. Autumn is coming early.
The ground is strewn with plums that are rotting
where they fall amongst the maggoty apples,
and the leaves that are blushing into decay.

Creak by arduous creak upon the stairs,
you haunt me with the man that you once were
as laboriously, you are rasping through the days.
On your bad side, your stiffening hand is
contracting to a claw, and now, when I hold
you close to me, I feel your bones against my breast.

I thought the memories, that grew like lichens
intertwined, were permanent. But now you say
you rarely think of them, so mine are going too.
Your voice is a dry whisper, vanishing on a breath.
Under that press of sky, it's feeling colder. And
our world is growing smaller every day.

SOME PICTURES

LIPSTICK
I am a little girl, and this is my mother.
She is as beautiful as a fashion plate.
Her lipstick is always fresh
and her hair is curled in shiny rows,
but her face is sad.
If I question her
she says, *it's just like that.*

LEMON CURD SANDWICHES
I'm all grown up and
now she is in our kitchen.
My baby was born dead
and she has come to help.
She cannot help.
She makes me lemon curd sandwiches.
You always liked those, she says.

CAKES
In her sheltered accommodation
we watch *The Cake Boss* together on TV.
And oh! The cakes are beautiful.
They are all she can remember, now.
Lovely cakes, like trees,
like castles, like handbags.
Her life has been eaten up.

THE NURSING HOME
But No, THIS is all she can remember.
I'm worried, she says. *I feel as if*
I don't know things and I should.
Do I know these people?
I pat her hand while I try not to see
her frightened eyes, while I tell her,
and tell me too: *everything's all right.*

Hieronymus Bosch -
Adoration of the Magi

My student halls were riddled with Bosch, done to tease.
Posters in every room, with monstrous heads gulping down
the melancholy sinners, who had reached Armageddon
with expressions of such sad surprise.

How unexpected then, this frozen tableau,
conventionally plonked in a wonky stable.
Perfunctory magi, dressed up in awkward party clothes,
with faces that have an air of going through the motions.

They appear as embarrassed as any strangers
shoved together by circumstance, exhibiting
the gaze avoidance that paralyses uncomfortable meetings.
Only the Christ child is looking, and he is a stiff little manikin.

His fingers are spread in an expression of denial or discomfort,
and he is held precariously by a frankly bovine mother,
pretty enough, but she, too, is sadly lacking in animation,
like the patient donkey at her side.

All the action is otherwise, for at the edges life is crowding in.
Sly-faced peasants have come to gawk, clambering
like monkeys over the rickety stable, dissolute, unimpressed,
as they peer at the impassive virgin and her child.

The servant in the corner stares with mild curiosity
at that pantomime dame, whose naked thigh protrudes
unpleasantly from his silks. He flourishes the crowns on his head
and in his hand, like cheap baubles for a Christmas tree.

Behind the bland patrons, and the saints they've commandeered,
a wolf is gobbling a man's head despite the knife inserted
in its back and a woman runs in horror from its mate.
Bands of horsemen ride at one another, though the capering peasants

on the left do not seem to see, and sheep graze safely on the hillsides.
Illusory cities shimmer in the distance where life is going on,
uninterrupted by the magical. Somewhere, everywhere, people
are dancing, people are dying, people are running, running, headlong

through life and into whatever death is waiting.
And possibly, improbably, salvation is in the picture here,
sifting riskily through the splayed fingers of that baby,
balanced in its mother's insubstantial grip.

The Adoration of the Magi in the Snow –
Pieter Bruegel the Elder

Yes, it's a cold coming.
And we see the true effort of it,
the baggage carts pulled by the extras
who never play much part
in filmic scenes like these.

And, as always, life is going on
beside this everyday miracle.
Men are breaking twigs for kindling,
the ice has been shattered
in the frozen river.

People are performing
the serious business of fetching water
and calling back that little girl,
who is sculling to and fro
on the treacherous surface.

Such innocent delight, though
a cross of lumber looms above her.
Soldiers are gathering beneath the
leafless branches where a magpie
perches with the other birds.

Sacks are carried past
the anomalous horses,
with their blinkers
and sumptuous apparel,
and attendants in their alien clothes.

Soldiers fold their arms against the cold
or incongruity of this - surely? -
God-forsaken place.
Dogs go as dogs do, with open faces
into whatever they are doing next.

And, in the ramshackle stable,
Joseph is slumped doubtfully against the wall.
Mary holds her baby to her, as any mother would,
and the kings are sinking to their knees,
spellbound, in the snow.

A haunting

It's like *The Woman in Black*. "Have you ever seen
a ghost?" I shake my head. I'm lying.
So I'll tell you my story.

And by the side of the bed.... I can't write it. It is
by the side of the bed, I can see it. Do I dream it?
I hope I am dreaming. Am I dreaming
with my eyes open, superimposing it on the everyday?

What is it? Who is it? It is the size of a small child.
It is the size of my small dead child, if the baby had grown.
Had she lived, had she breathed.

*(On an x-ray of a still born you can see it never drew
breath by the uninflated rib cage – so I'm told.)*

We are all ill. Me, my husband, and the children who are
climbing into our bed for comfort. Now they are fast asleep but
heat radiates from them and my hair is lank with their sweat.

So.... this is the story continuing, not as it should do. I'm back
at the beginning. I have crept from my bed and into my son's
which is cool now, with his absence. If I lie on my left side
I can see the landing, and all the doors. The carpet stretches out.

*It is a nasty green but we have not afforded to replace it yet.
The walls are another horrid green which clashes though surely greens
should tone together? They don't. Olive and mint, mint and olive.*

It is "an infelicitous mixture" – I think I have stolen this from
a book of Ruth Rendell's where Chief Inspector Wexford is looking
at beans and fish fingers on a plate. "An infelicitous mixture," he thinks.

But I digress, because I don't want to look at it again.

It is, as I said before, the size of a small child. It is a girl of 6 or 7.
I know it is a girl. I don't know how or why I know this, and you
will see why that is puzzling when I can bring myself to tell you.

I am lying on my left side and the nasty green carpet
continues to stretch itself out between the doors. And between
the carpet and the doors, and between my door and my son's bed
in which I am trying to sleep, she stands by the bed.

But she is draped from head to foot in sleek black satin.
It is dropped over her head as if she is a piece of furniture covered
in a lustrous cloth. It moulds itself over the round dome of her skull,
so she is a shape, a black shape, with a dull gleam to its
black covering, which falls from the dome of her skull to the floor.

And that's it.
Someone said I was feverish.
And the Methodist Minister at the poetry group said,
"Perhaps it was a demon?"
and someone pushes him hard in the ribs to shut him up.

Let's move on. "Has anybody ever seen a ghost?"

A Love Story

It was 1970.

We walked beside the river, hand in hand, and the sun
gilded us, and I was dazzled by the blackness of your hair,
your golden skin, and the amber of your eyes, sometimes
black as olives in the glinting dark. When I look back
it is always summer, and your skin is hot against mine,
breast to breast, in the half shadows where my hair falls over
us in a silky veil. We both remember the short green dress,
brighter than the grass, cheap polyester from C&A, sticky
with the heat. And when I took it off it was rust marked
where the buckle of its belt had rested on my waist.

And you ask, and I ask myself, what is the point of all this?
And that *is* the point. A day burnished until it gleams.
Two young people, hand in hand, beside a river sequined
with sun so bright you had to squint to see. I don't write
love poetry, my poetry is full of the darkness that followed,
but this is a love poem, that has walked into my head and
surprised us both.

Hidden Changes

Here I am slotted into the secret space behind the houses,
walking in the fine silt of a reclaimed sea bed, and
the farty smell of cabbages scents the air. Men are waiting
for the carousel, where the vegetables are cut and
carried to the trailer in bright red cups.

As they move for the dog and me to pass one smiles,
pretends to hide the long knife that he carries in his jacket,
and I smile back. To be honest, they are usually just figures
from the car. Harvesting the sprouts, in fog and ice,
sitting side by side behind the tractors, dropping

brassica seedlings into place, sometimes bunching armfuls
of daffodils. Working hard. In the town, they are invisible
until they speak. Language crowding the air, Lithuanian, Latvian,
Estonian, Polish. And new names, *Basia's Pantry, Baltic Food,
Romanian Shop, Europe Express,* line the busy streets.

A vodka still blows up in an industrial unit. In the paper, some
of the petty criminals and bad drivers have foreign names.
A friend says *I'm not racist, but…* at a dinner party. But, but, but.
In a generation, the children will have vanished, them to us,
their accents gone, only surnames remaining.

Back and back – Dutch drainage engineers, rubble
of Norman Castles, Roman salt pans, humping up out of
the ripening wheat. And more recently, and less forgettably,
the sombre, indigestible, 1930s and the 40s, when people
fled here, refugees from the claws of history.

Mary

There's another shouter at the nursing home.
Her face is a little walnut of rage and maybe
bewilderment at where she's ended up.
"I wanna wee wee," she says. Every ten
minutes. "I'm going to gush." she says.
And "I'm bored. Take me somewhere.
Take me to bed." She says. Over and over
and over again. Over again.

The quiet ladies move a little in their special
chairs that help them up onto the walking frames
- so they can dodder off to who knows where.
They are not quite bad enough to transfer
to the other house – yet – where the residents are
all are wrapped up in their casings
of confusion and repetition. Shouting and
banging. Banging and shouting.

And suddenly the quiet ladies are back.
Their eyes have woken up and malice is glowering
from their crinkled faces. They all scowl at Mary
Even Lily, who has a cloud of white curls
framing her tranquil face, is frowning now.
Others are muttering to one another;
spite spiders itself over their faces, turning them back
into the mean girls that they once were.

What's left then?

What's left then?
We know each other
better than you can know.
We can still
make each other laugh,
forgive what needs
forgiving.
But it's lonely as the silences
grow longer, the exhaled breath
gives out before the sentence ends.
The future contracts.
I look at my mother, emptied by time,
In the nursing home and don't wish that
On either of us.
Today I read about a suicide pact
and, for a moment, I was tempted.

My memories lie broken at your feet

My memories lie broken at your feet
now that your graceless days unreel
and your lovely face has fallen.

I look into your so-familiar eyes hoping,
though not really hoping,
to catch something of you whisking
out of sight. I want to ask who's in there?
But I already know the answer.

I remember Woolworth's biscuits, iced
in pink and acid yellow, chocolate brown,
and how, when you dunked them in your tea,
the surface crazed and crazed across
yet never broke apart.

Wild blackberries - a sonnet

It's hot. We are walking in an old quarry
that has given itself back to knapweed, scabious,
the bright ox-eye daisies. Amongst the transitory
grasses, black eyes wink back at us.

It's strange how memory suddenly lets go,
and unfurls its secrets, still intact.
The sight, the smell, the sound of each slow
moment is returned without a lapse or lack.

It's all there. The soft resistance of the fruit,
between the teeth and then upon the tongue
the sudden sensual letdown of the juice.
How short that day - although it seemed so long.

If I could bottle it, somehow preserve that rush,
then I could say that this is what remains of us.

Today it is Christmas Day and the phone rang early.

The nurses pull the curtains back and the windows
frame the charcoal calligraphy of trees, and the lawn
is banded with December sun. The sky is luminous,
white and grey stripes across that incessant blue
which always lies behind the clouds.
Improbably a blackbird – a thrush? – is singing.

The complicated estuaries of veins on her chest
echo the patterns of the scribbled branches
and I think, *how beautiful she was,* and look for
the shapely bones beneath the skin, which is shrivelled
and folded now. She asks for a drink and coughs,
plucking at her chest, but then she is quiet,
the breath rising and falling with a catch.

In the dining room I can hear the snap of crackers
and chatter about hats; the Christmas lunch rattles in
on its trolley. 5 days ago, we were at the party there,
singing along to sixties hits.

There is no way back from this. It could be now,
it could be tomorrow or the day after, but she is dying.
It's like a staircase and she is moving away from me,
step by inevitable step, and I am thinking
please don't die on Christmas Day. Though there
will of course be deaths and births like
any other day, and on *this* day after all we celebrate
a baby laid out, ready, on an altar.

Later her breath has subsided to an intermittent gasp.
She no longer speaks or drinks or looks at me. But
she squeezes my hand. *Tell her about her Christmas
presents, she will hear you.* So, like a magician's act,
I run her fingers over the brushed fabric of the nightie,
her silky scarf, spray perfume in the air and hate
myself for hating my inadequate performance.

And then I hold her hand and stroke her hair and tell her that
I love her, and my brother and sister are coming soon.
I photograph her thumb pressed against my hand and think
I will need to see this. Later I'm reading *Lincoln in the Bardo*
on my phone, a tale of graveyards so a stupid choice.
I doubt I will return to it precipitately.

Larkin said *days are where you live* but she will die
in this one. Slipping away, silently, just as I have turned
my back, to drink black coffee that the nurse has brought.

The Lovely Bones

I had been there before, at a bedside, where she was choked
with infection. And death hovered over a chest that couldn't rise
and fall, then death just slinked away. Like Lazarus, she always rose.
We laughed and said she was immortal and waited for the telegram.
But this time she died.

People used to say to her, *"You'll make lovely bones"*.
She was always beautiful, with long hands. And feet she hated
because she always thought they were too big, next to the aunts
with their tiny shoes. Now her graceful hand is lying on the bed
and for one last time I take it in mine.

At the funeral the Minister puts on charisma like a coat of
many colours. Sincerity fills the air. It is all quiet, gentle, shaped to
calm. He puts his hand upon her coffin lid, where the rain has left
precarious drops amongst the flowers. And he is entrusting her now
to the cold ground.

Yet at the house the Minister was quiet and grey, wearing his own
shrouded distance and I realised that he made appearances,
and then the magic came. So here was a dilemma for him. Dementia.
Had my mother's soul fled along with her memory?
Or would it hover? Or was it silenced, deep inside her?

I hoped, as I always hope, for the numinous, the astonishing, the
touch of God, tipping over the everyday, like tables. That some-
where my mum was whole again, not just dropped into that dark slot.
That Vicars had answers, not this silence while he wondered
what to say. He said it was hard to imagine how that could work.

and that his faith had kind of weakened over time.
It rained and rained We threw roses and wet mud on the coffin lid,
heels sinking in the ground, and everywhere the silly umbrellas
bobbed about. And, as foolishly as them, I like to think she is some-
where, with her mother and the aunts. Drinking tea and reminiscing.

Whole again.

Vija Celmin's Starfield

I'm thinking of your mezzotints: your infinite patience
as you add mark on mark. The rocker moves
and dark on dark and dot by dot the constellations
grow to pinpricks on bright white paper.

Here on Skye it is all water. Which holds the sky and
holds the unmoving mountains with their distant crags,
where eagles circle and display, developing from black dots
against the brightness of the clouds.

When the sun shines, silvery mica glistens
on the stony outcrops, while in the loch the water is
opaque. All the reflections are gone now and,
in the glitter of its surface, galaxies are moving,
winking in and out, like a desolate cosmos.
Mirroring those lonely depths, beyond the sky.

Rondel

The meadow is awash with flowers
and bees and butterflies stud the grass.
Like every day, this too will pass
and fall into the darkness of lost hours.

So, what to do? Just say this day is ours:
it is a day that others can't surpass.
The meadow is awash with flowers
and bees and butterflies stud the grass.

Memory itself has such a power
That, even though the loveliness can't last,
each year the flowers return, and they forecast

that a remembered day will never sour.
The meadow is awash with flowers
and bees and butterflies stud the grass.

Christmas Days

It's Christmas Day and, like every day,
there will be births with all their pains,
until the snuffling pink babies are laid out
in such ordinary mangers.

If it is true, there was a Christmas Day
with a birth and a death divined.
Such a vulnerable sacrifice placed
upon the altar of the day.

If it is true, it is the biggest gift
to live and die in days, like us,
and refuse the magician's cloak
which would snap it all away in a

thunderclap. And in its place just hang
there, a man and not a man, yet die
like us. Disarming the powerful
with such a clever sleight of hand.

Selected Poems
1982-2016

Stillbirth

Poor hollowhead,
I talk to you in your walnut sleep
but your face forgets to move: in my
arms I hold a stranger
with voracious eyes,
wound in your yellowed shawl.
Such a thin tissue
between sleep and waking,
presence and absence:
in dreams I presented you
to roomfuls of strangers.
Now I'm talking to you
but, bone-quiet, you do not answer.
Poor hollowhead,
this is your sister,
who sleeps less quietly,
and in your place.

The Still Room

All year the room grew drowsy
with slow mouth-music, breathing
through fermentation locks.

After the sunlight, the air
was iced beneath the trees.

Lace overflowed the trugs:
odd flat-faced elderflowers, then
their must, feline in the darkness.
Drugged bees of yeast rose until
the jars thickened to pale honey.

The year closed on button eyes,
glittering from the elderbranches;
the royal purple of their juices.
Then heartbeats, and the soft curd,
gathering like sleep. Slowly
shadow fingers bubbled into sight,
semaphoring through the glass.

It lies on its side now, that year,
siphoned and sealed in pied rows -
Tyrian and straw-gold brimming
with another spring, another autumn.
And out beyond these racks,
new seasons, splintered faces -
smashed glass, smashed glass.

The bottles chink together;
their throats are stopped
and growing tired of waiting.

The Mouths

The long sigh fogs the mirror,
and that big 'O' of sky
is gathered to the tunnel vision
of the contents of a blink.
The eelwet fens are filling.
The thick air drips where skittled trees
show their brown bones, their dark feet
in the litter of all that autumn coinage.

Only the grey road persists;
its sudden disclosures.
Ahead, behind,
the white mouth swallows it all:
the scaffolding of the tractor,
the clamps, the cauliflower sheep.

When the car stops
your veiled smile fills my window,
and a coat as grey as mist.
I know at once that I, too,
will button my fogs around me
and shut you out.

Nexus

This road as string,
landmarks twisting it to knots.

All the houses stay behind to
drown in saturated fields. Instead
pot-bellied cooling towers balance
on these stilts, and slop their
induced currents in the Trent.
Now tower blocks are straddling
entrances and exits: hanging
windows on the dark, the little
tapers held to say "we're here".
A TV mast blinks on and off,
strange legerdemain to conjure
disbelief with all its absences.

And in between balletic cartwheels,
then the cooling belly of the car.
Such a dark knot on these banal
fields, such an altered landscape.

A Cartographer's Anniversary

Twelve chartless years
sheeted in bridal mists, making maps.

Seas like polished mirrors.
Taking soundings on the breathing swell,
licking the spindrift salt
of rocks that come and go;
slick seals' heads laced in foam.
Voyages round your granite definitions,
the veiled obsidian face, reflective:
my ragged coasts and briny estuaries.
Bone islands. Land bridges.

Expeditions to the lush interior,
where tongues twist, sense fails:
we make translations.

This is a love story:
now the maps are drawn.

The Body Book

My child is two and talks to me:
'The shell-head in my body'. He means
his skull, tucked tight and white.

'Bang your head, you'll feel it.' Now
he laughs to hear his fingers drum.

And though I join him, I can hear
the sound of salt-fresh water running
out, out, out, leaving weary nothings.

Tide-wrack and this heavy, silted head.

Gap in the Rails

(for my father, d. 1963)

You are a closed gate; a path
strung with barbed wire.
You are the broken fingerpost.
You are a space on the map
where cartography has failed,
a landscape I shall never see.

You are a strait of water
I cannot cross. Seabirds wheel
and cry there, their throats
make such empty noises...
Sandbanks shift and change
with the drag of the tide.

You are the mountain
no-one will climb,
glacier-smooth, featureless,
its handholds gone.
You are a shrouded summit,
lost in cloud.

You are the missed connection,
the train that disappears
with a blink into the tunnel,
its whistle trailing
rags of sound behind...
You are the gap in the rails.

Oubliette

I shall never know what brought me here.
A careless word? Some act? Then a hand
across my mouth as quiet as velvet
cloaked me from the light.
Now I am quite forgotten,
swaddled and suspended, mute.
Sun stripes across the room from day
to night then back to day again.
Flies drive themselves to death against the panes.
My gaolers never come. My notes are lost,
filed by some technician since dismissed.
Who will ever call me? Make it soon.
I yearn to feel the kiss of true attention,
even as it cleaves my dumb head from my neck.

Green men

Who are the green men, grinning from church walls,
sprouting leaves and paganism? They hide
in church porches, walls and misericords, peer out
by window frames; catch our eyes with a glint
of old malice, carved from stone and wood and
craftsmanship.

Perhaps they are a whispering of an older religion,
where wells were dressed, and broken swords made
moments of crazed reflection in the bright water.
Then were swallowed. Holly berries and mistletoe,
incongruous, suggestive, still wink at us from
Christmas cards.

And always there are visions of the green youth dying
in the corn, and of the resurrected god. There when
Helston has its furry dance and Mari Lwyd, the
skull faced hobby horse, capers on that bridge,
and surely when the deermen put on their antlers,
line up in rows, and dance.

The Scarecrow Christ

The fields are flat and brown, it's hard to think
they'll ever stand high with corn, flare with rape
again this summer. For now the scarecrows lurch
at crazy angles. They trail old coats and rags.
Polythene bags flap around the suggestions of
their shoulders. And yet the wind lifts
their shoddy clothes and they are touched with
magic; they always seem about to fly.

It's Sunday and I've taken you to Chapel.
Everything is grey and earnest. There's no
incense here, though a sense of well-meaning
sifts gently through the air. I don't think I belong.
It's Lent and the sermon is all about temptation.
I feel I would not pass those tests. Now I see
distraction in the corner of my eyes; a painting.
When I can, I take a picture on my phone.

It shows me strips of cloth, snarled around
an empty cross, a tenuous fabric
lifting in air currents, tangled with light.
Something. Nothing. Faith, elusive as a sigh.
A scarecrow pinned to a stick.
Leaning forwards, with the wind stirring its tatters.
And always on the point of alteration,
by some sudden unexpected angle of the sun.

Magpies

I am driving where the ambulance has driven
though much more quietly of course.
And, as I drive, I greet the magpies that I pass
and ask about their families. While rooks
arrange themselves in trees, like books
on shelves.

At the hospital you are OK but
the woman in the next bed is not so lucky.
The heart care nurse, the trauma nurse
and several doctors are crowding round her X-ray.

And they are laughing - not maliciously -
in the way you laugh when actually you're shocked.
Apparently, it's a really odd aneurysm.
Like nothing they have ever seen before.

Sprouts

In my first winter in a substituted house
swollen green knuckles crack
off arthritic stems.
There are sprouts to pick.
In the kitchen bowl the green heads bob,
with ageing mummy faces
wrapped in dishonest shrouds.
My fingernails fret at the honed necks
and the years are peeled away.
Nan's hands stir in the water ...
estuaries of blue veins writhe beneath her skin.
She shouts at me
because I pare her sprouts to nothing,
searching for the kernel, the clarified centre.

Gift-Wrapped

Marshalled, stiff-legged as the turkey,
on a long route to our dinner -
this was a paper day; all wrapped up.
We've been wearing faces unaccustomed as
our clothes, stiff-jawed from bonhomie.

All day the drifts of paper came to rest with
autumn rustles by the skirting boards The
children, sick with sweets and novelty lay
silted on the sofas. We carried them as
precious parcels to the car.

Orion and his dog are gone elsewhere, the
candles quite snuffed out. Now our car
stutters in a whitened space in which mist
tissues float towards us; the last
unwrappings, sheet on sheet.

The Packhorse Trail to Glossop

In the morning we sit and watch his parents:
they are yellowing as leaves will do, this October.
Mortality is walking sticks, rows of medicine,
polythene on chairs. But we can leave

those rooms behind - where clocks will tick
themselves to silence, sooner or later,
strangers will wash two lifetimes clean away –
and drive through Sheffield into Ladybower.

Purpose drowned, the packhorse trail has unmade itself.
Conifers lie like a rug across the hill and reflect
only themselves in the reservoir's calm surface;
the woods creak with wrens, shrill with goldcrest.

Above the trees, clouds thread our hair.
There is nothing here but the blind stutter
of a lost plane. We have unloosed ourselves,
though, like October, evening is on its way.

A sign post is pointing into mist.
Obediently, the children follow. Christopher analyses
the viscosity and depth of mud, Jon stings nettles
back, drops boots and drizzles at the sky,

and, sitting on the stile, Imogen is gone already.
Below, the city beats like a restless heart,
threatening to leave her stranded here with us.
So, finger by finger, she has removed herself.

Anybody's

Saturday, and the night has wound them up
and set them going. Those pretty girls!
They stream across the bridge, tinsel and brittle,
into the jaws of the doorman: what a smile!

Linda's hair is a cliché of gossamer, alchemy
of disco lights transmutes each filament.
A world of mirrored fragments dances
across the floor. How wet her eyes are-
they lick the room, get its taste,
while she moves to music she doesn't hear.
Tonight, he will entertain her.

White wine shivers in her glass, sweet
("See her? She's anybody's.
Sitting legs apart like that")
as she is. All he sees is her pointed tongue,
the lip-sticked smile, her soft heat,
the openings and closings of that wet mouth.
What wouldn't he do?

Outside, his arm closes round her shoulders
in the woolly dark, and their drinks
bump them together while they walk. Cheers!

As they cross the bridge, her effervescence
is dying on him. Until, a coping stone above
disaster, he dances lightly on the parapet,
("He'd had a few; although I laughed,
I told him to come . . .") down
to a dark nothing of water way below,
and its black mouth, opening to receive him.

Sweet Briar

Roses hung on the wire of her voice;
she wore dresses of creaseless silk
cracked from the tight cases of nuts.
She was shuttered, until that old lady
wound her tale. The bloody spindle turned.

Then she was sealed in a room darkened
with the tendrils of thorns and the hush
of the pointed leaves, where roses
with close red hearts, curled, secretive,
studded branches, thick as her arms, with blood.

Her eyes were blind to the froth of the sky,
seething and changing in the window's square.

And when she was woken, she was quite lost
to her apple-yellow sisters, lost
to the quiet song of their voices.

He has kissed her neck, her shoulders,
bites her throat. Now she has ripened
into his dark fruit, rich and sticky,
and the key in the lock has turned her
secret, compliant, thornless.

Old Men

The old men queue in crooked rows.
Their swollen fingers swipe
and miss the golden litter;
it falls and binds their ankles.
You're crying as your feet have gone,
locked in the same bright fetters
that rustle thinly as you walk.
Your face hardens to an old man's yell.

Now grandfather's hands
signal their inflamed semaphore,
and knot round your soft palms.
Yet young and blue and bright,
in his eyes a lizard darts
out to the graveyard garden,
where his stumbling neighbour
kicks yellow leaves, scattering wits.

Strandline

The wind stalks the salt-marsh.
Pale sedges bow and scrape to a fractured sky
which shivers in the water-stands.
The fluted dunes are seeded -
with rabbit droppings, thrush anvils;
small cemeteries of snails.

A redshank triple chinks its danger.
Her head is turning, but beside her he is still,
with an emptied face, blank as water.
Skylarks rise and fall, rise and fall -
she tells him, "those could be on wires".
Her words are snatched away
and side by side they move like marionettes
where blackthorn roots clench the sand.

The landscape is encoded in an idiom of signs -
here an opened gull's egg, there one fraying wing,
beached in the stranded mermaids' purses.
The sea is just a smear. "Do you recall...?"
The memories shimmer briefly,
but beneath their feet the transient dunes
are sifting through the marram strands,
and they're wearing different faces now.

Stubble Burning

Spilling hot beads across the field
I balanced the fire on a pitchfork
to shake it out, little by little.

Then it was animal, running from us,
quickly, quickly. Cracking our ears
with the sound of its feet, urgent

through the stubble. Where its black
prints showed the white smoke thinned,
darkened. And the sky, obliterate.

You, too, running ahead of me. 'Think
what you're doing, lad!' Thickened air,
dancing with charred pepper. I would

consume... Next there was a slow grey
sky, something soft, with velvet
and violet in it. The stubble blued

and trailed with lines of ash. And in
the dusk white eyes of fire, blinking
at the smoke that stings to tears.

How you turned and said 'not you,
you're too...' You laughed. As if I
couldn't fail to understand. And yet

came spring, the corn half grown, my
tongue flickered on your body. Until
you burned, arching in the tractor ruts.

You asking 'have you met my bit of rough?'
Speculative eyes and laughter, my hands
and feet grown bigger. Something burning.

The sky consumed in black. I stayed behind
and watched the fires, transformed to
chains of party lights across the field.

Out for Sunday Tea

It's only a bus ride —
then I'm back in that dusk-dark garden
where martins scream of leaving
and rowan berries splash the path.
My cousin and I are anyone we want.
There's the vinegar taste of salmon,
and the sweet geometry of fruit from tins.
The grown-ups talk and drink their tea
while our eyes prickle into roundness
in the darkening panes. "Pretend that I'm…"
But it's almost time to go.
At home, my uniform rustles in the wardrobe.
Stiff and uncompromising,
it knows better who I have to be.

I call back once.
My daughter walks the unfamiliar lawns
and watches her changing face
in a pond that wasn't there. "Sorry."
We didn't make the wedding and my cousin's gone.
My aunt displays a hanger; a white discarded dress.
I try to fill it out —
but she could be anyone if I met her now.
We grown-ups talk and drink our tea.

One of those women who

She was painting the reflected water
lapping her brother's soft cheek –
the colour washes there,
coming and going as the whim of the sea.
At his back, the Atlantic crashed:
long fingers, black basalt intrusions,
broke the waves to surf.
He floated brittle stars in rock pools.
"Watch him! Watch him!" her mother cried,
like some ill-starred bird, a petrel,
dirty-feathered, promising storms.
His brain was dashed in the surge
of her birth waters…

"My boy, my pretty boy," his mother sang,
"Why should it be you?" Then: "Keep him safe."
So he was at her shoulder, as an albatross.
So he crawled into her head at night.
So he entered her pictures to haunt
their surfaces: the pigments
scabbed on the palette, disuse
stiffened in the brushes, cemented
the lids of tubes in place. She turned
and ran.

Now she takes trains and cars across
Europe; fills her body, without meaning,
with the bodies of men and her head
with a gallery she cannot display.
Leaving just one canvas – the water
dancing, dancing, on his face,
empty in the spindrift.

The Stranger Story

Has been waiting to be told.
How his ashes were tucked,
secretly, into the crooked heart
of the apple tree.

Each spring the blossom fell,
like weddings, on to the grass
where violets lifted their foxed faces
and the stream talked to itself,
repeating its memories;
senile babbling. And he moved
into the creaking joints of the tree,
the bark boxed him, he became nothing
but an imperfection in the wood.
A knot, a flaw: splintering.

Later, children grow there
to scatter petals on the wind,
make cairns of the hard green beads
of aborted fruit under the tree,
kick the wasp-brewed yeast of windfalls,
rake dried leaves through their fingers –
and each winter, climb its bare limbs.

Acknowledgments

Poems were published in Poetry Nottingham, 1984, *Sprouts*; Faber & Faber Poetry Introduction 6, 1985, *Strandline, Stillbirth, The Still Room, The Mouths;* Six: The Versewagon Poetry Manual, 1985, *Nexus, Gift Wrapped, Stubble Burning, Out for Sunday Tea, A Cartographer's Anniversary, The Body Book;* Ambit 107, 1987, *Sweet Briar;* Hanging Windows On The Dark, Wide Skirt Press, 1987, *Nexus, Gift Wrapped;* Poetry Matters, Journal Of Peterloo Poets, No 5, 1987, Open Poetry Competition 1987, (Highly Commended),*Anybody's*; Prospice 20 1987, *Old Men, One of Those Women Who*; Critical Quarterly, Summer 1988, *The Stranger Story*; Wide skirt Issue 7 1988, *The Packhorse Trail to Glossop;* Anvil New Poets 1990, *Stubble Burning, Out for Sunday Tea;* Outside The Chain Of Hands, Big Little Poem Books, 1994, *Gap in the Rails;* Behind the Glass 2012, redplantpress, *Oubliette, Green men, The Scarecrow Christ*; Poetry of Hospitals and Waiting Rooms, redplantpress, 2013, *Magpies;* The North, no 52, spring 2014 *Several Tests of Dementia Severity**; The Blue Max Review 2015, Fermoy Poetry Festival Anthology, *The Lady Chapel and the Virgin*; DE4/A1 The Templar Anthology 2016, *Tell it to the Bees, Dr White*, Southlight 23, Spring 2018, *Full Cold Moon on Christmas Eve, Some Pictures, Autumn is Coming, A Love Story, Mary*; May 2018 Acumen 91 *Hidden Changes* (I also read this on Boston Calling, a BBC Radio 4 production, hosted by Benjamin Zephaniah, August 2017).

Biography

Shirley Bell is the editor of The Blue Nib, a growing online literary magazine and small publisher (www.magazine.thebluenib.com), and she is a widely published and anthologised poet. Her poetry is archived in the Special Collection in the University of Lincoln's Library and, as a result, she has collected together all her published poetry from 1982 to early 2016 in her book, *Dark is a Way and Light is a Place.* The Wide Skirt published her pamphlet *Hanging Windows on the Dark.* She has published two other pamphlets, *behind the glass* and *Poetry of Hospitals and Waiting Rooms.* She has been writing poetry since the 1980s and has read widely all over the country. She worked as a Writer in Residence with all ages, from primary to students in Higher Education. She was Literature Consultant for Lincolnshire and Humberside Arts and edited their magazine, *Proof.*

www.ingramcontent.com/pod-product-compliance
Lightning Source LLC
Chambersburg PA
CBHW060049050426

42448CB00011B/2366